The Bartender's Assistant

The Bartender's Assistant

A Guide for the Journey

by Tony Blair

A Study Guide for
The Bartender: A Fable about a Journey

by Mike McNichols

RESOURCE *Publications* • Eugene, Oregon

THE BARTENDER'S ASSISTANT
A Guide for the Journey

Resource Publications
An Imprint of Wipf and Stock Publishers
199 W. 8th Ave., Suite 3
Eugene, OR 97401

www.wipfandstock.com

ISBN 13: 978-1-49825-608-3

Manufactured in the U.S.A.

Contents

Foreword

WHEN I began writing *The Bartender* as part of a doctoral project at George Fox Evangelical Seminary, I found that I was not prepared for the difficulty I encountered in writing fiction. Academic writing is one thing—there's no character development, no plot line, no dialogue to follow. But fiction demands all that and more. It can be just as messy and troublesome as life itself, which is why it works well when we're talking about the mission of the church in the world. If you want messy and troublesome, the life of the church has more than its share.

The Bartender was intended for an audience of people who appreciate academic speculation but also hunger for fleshing things out in everyday life. It's one thing to talk about spiritual formation and evangelism as issues embedded within both ecclesiology and missiology; it's another to engage in those things for oneself and with one's neighbor, especially a neighbor who seems broken beyond repair. Putting the roughness and uncertainty of these things into the lives of frail, struggling, fictional (sort of) characters was my way of helping draw people into the conversation and, hopefully, more deeply into God's mission in the world.

My friend Tony Blair has taken my modest enterprise and created this wonderful study guide to help leaders and churches open up conversations about both the inward and outward life of the church. He has taken the jumbled furniture of my fictional house and offered a framework for a sense of order—not in the way that confines, but in the creative, intelligent way that he has for preparing things for movement and action. I'm grateful for his thoughtful work that has resulted in this study guide.

Both of us agree that spiritual formation—the formation of a person's inner life by the work of God's Spirit—and evangelism are not only important but also indispensable in the life of the church. However, we also share the conviction that both of those areas of life require new explorations and innovative engagements. We don't intend to throw any babies out with the bath water; we're more interested in finding the babies in the midst of very murky water, and helping them to grow and flourish.

Tony and I journeyed together with Leonard Sweet and a wonderful group of learners for three years, exploring questions about life, ministry, the church, and the world. That time of growth and learning moved us into new areas of thought in a number of cherished areas of our Christian faith. We both share the hope that others will not only join in the discussion, but will also engage those around them in the larger conversation that takes place around the table of Jesus.

Michael McNichols
Lent 2010

PREFACE

About *The Bartender* . . .

Christian faith is continually challenged by the tension between certainty and mystery. A historic faith can seem threatened by the uncomfortable recognition that God continues to work in a rapidly changing culture. *The Bartender* is a fable about the messiness and unpredictability of lives being opened up to God through relationships characterized by deep listening and looking for the ongoing work of God in the world. The parallel and sometimes intersecting paths of two men on different spiritual journeys reveal how God seems to be present in the most scandalous of human dramas. When both men take risks that threaten their own religious sensibilities, they find new ways of living out the implications of their faith.

—From the Back Cover

About *The Bartender's Assistant*

THIS STUDY guide was created chapter by chapter as the staff of Hosanna! A Fellowship of Christians in Lititz, Pennsylvania, read and discussed this fascinating book twice a month over a period of ten months. As we read further, we found ourselves handing out copies to members of our congregation and others, for the issues we were discussing were so relevant to so much of our other conversations about life, ministry, spiritual formation, evangelism, relationships, and the life. And Mike McNichol's choice to discuss these issues in the context of a fable made them accessible in ways that a more didactic approach would not have.

As a result, this guide has been adapted for the use of a more general audience. Specifically, it's been formatted into 12 sessions for those who would wish to read, discuss it, and practice its principles together over a defined period of time. Of course, it can be adapted for other schedules and formats. Whether you're reading this on your own or as part of a group, I hope it's helpful to you.

—Tony Blair

Session 1

The Prologue

. . . in which we discover that we are reading a story about regrets.

"Do nothing without deliberation, but when you have acted, do not regret it" (Sirach 32:19).

1. Who or what is Sirach?

2. "People who lack religious affinities can embrace regret once they recognize that something is horribly wrong with the world and there is no solution to be found" (p. viii). Do you agree that unreligious people believe that there is no solution? What if they believe religion is what is horribly wrong with the world?

3. What is your understanding of God's will? Read Romans 12:2 and then answer the question again.

4. Have you ever felt that God was being deceptive? That He is an astonished and secretive parent? That what the Bible says about Him "just doesn't work?" How have you navigated through that experience? How could you help another?

5. What hopes or concerns do you have about reading a "story about regrets?"

Chapter 1

. . . in which we meet Pastor Paul Philips and
Music City Community Church.

*"I saw all the deeds that are done under the sun; and see, all
is vanity and a chasing after the wind" (Ecclesiastes 1:14).*

1. Do you share Pastor Paul's concern about "transfer growth" as opposed to the evangelization of new Christians?

2. What kind of church is necessary to effectively reach those who are unchurched? Can an existing church do that, or does one need to start from scratch with a church plant?

3. Think about the exchange between Paul and Ralph in light of the believer's dual commitment to authentic community and effective outreach. Can a church do both effectively or must one suffer in order to serve the other?

4. Who is ultimately responsible for caring for the insiders? For reaching the outsiders?

5. Is it a good or bad thing when people leave a church? How can you tell the difference?

6. Is it harder to reach the unchurched now, in this generation, than it was in the past? If yes, why is our message not resonating?

7. What counsel would you give Pastor Paul at the end of Chapter 1?

Session 2

Chapter 2

... in which we discover how Paul ended up becoming
a pastor, of all things.

*"Paul, thou art beside thyself; much learning doth
make thee mad" (Acts 26:24, KJV).*

1. "Paul Philips often felt like a like spiritual misfit" (p. 6). He
   didn't feel like he belonged in church ministry. Have you
   ever felt the same way?

2. Was being part of the ministry staff of a church ever part of
   your plans or hopes for your life?

3. Where have you felt or seen the "celebrity" syndrome Paul
   was captivated by?

4. How easy or difficult do you think it is for someone with "depth and integrity" (like Dr. Grayson) to survive in a denominational setting? Why?

5. Do you ever feel like church life gets caught up in stupid, picky things . . . like the locations of the piano and organ in the sanctuary?

6. Pastor Paul had a growing conviction that "following after this ever-present, ever-working God was the most important thing in the world" (p. 10). How does "following after" God differ from other approaches to ministry?

Chapter 3

. . . in which we discover why Paul loved his church.

"It is grace, nothing but grace, that we are allowed to live in community with Christian brethren" (Dietrich Bonhoeffer).

1. How does the architecture of a place of worship affect our feelings about the space? Is there a kind of building that feels more like "church" to you?

2. How does the arrangement of the furniture and equipment in a place of worship reflect its theology?

3. Pastor Paul resonated with Rembrandt's "Return of the Prodigal Son." If you can, find and take a good look at that painting. (You can find it online at http://www.rembrandt-painting.net/rmbrndt_1655-1669/prodigal_son.htm.) What does it provoke within you?

4. What other images or paintings convey grace or are otherwise spiritually significant to you?

5. How can or do we use visual images to reinforce our own faith?

6. Pastor Paul connected the smell of coffee with his congregation. What smells do you associate with worship? With fellowship?

7. How can or do we use smell and the other senses to reinforce our own faith?

8. "With all its quirks and weaknesses, Paul loved this church." Have you felt that way about your church? A group thereof? Why?

Chapter 4

. . . in which Paul and his leadership team meet at a local pub.

"If you would be a real seeker after truth, it is necessary that at least once in your life you doubt, as far as possible, all things" (Rene Descartes).

1. In this chapter we meet two other members of Paul's leadership team: Gracie and Dean. Forgetting their demographic characteristics (age, ethnicity, gender) for a moment, do you see in them any representation of church leaders you know? Anything of yourself?

2. How do you see spiritual formation relating to evangelism?

Session 3

Chapter 5

... in which we get to know a recovering alcoholic and a troubled waitress.

"Look, a glutton and a drunkard, a friend of tax collectors and sinners! Yet wisdom is vindicated by her deeds"
(Matthew 11:19).

1. Emil is a recovering alcoholic serving drinks in a bar. Our minds probably jump fairly quickly into "judgment mode" when reading this. What do you think or feel about Emil's choices?

2. What does Angie need?

3. What does Emil have to offer her ... or others?

Chapter 6

... in which Paul, Dean, and Gracie discuss evangelism
... and Angie.

*"The church with no great anguish on its heart has no
great music on its lips" (Karl Barth).*

1. To what anguish is Barth referring? What music emerges
   from this anguish?

2. Dean introduces Paul and Gracie to spiritual direction.
   He recommends Thomas Merton's *Spiritual Direction and
   Meditation*, noting that Merton describes spiritual direction
   as "joint effort between two Christians where one talks and
   the other listens. . . . It's about helping someone respond
   to what God is doing" (p. 26). Have you encountered the
   Merton book? Would you agree with his description of
   spiritual direction?

3. Dean also recommends *The Starbridge Series* by Susan
   Howatch. Have you encountered this series? If so, would
   you recommend it? Why?

4. Dean suggests that spiritual direction may be one way to go about the business of evangelism, a way that is more natural than the programming that many churches attempt. What do you think? Why does he suggest this?

5. "What if, instead of looking for people who want to sit still for our pre-recorded message, our role as Christians was to pay attention to the people around us, to look for what God is already doing, and then help people recognize that? What if our role was to cooperate with God instead of expecting God to cooperate with our programs?" (p. 27). Is it all one or the other? A dichotomy? Where is God at work in the world? What do you make of Gracie's confession on page 28?

6. And, finally, what about Angie? Paul asks about her: "Do you see signs of God being at work?"

Chapter 7

. . . in which we hear a bit of Angie's story.

"Hope deferred makes the heart sick" (Proverbs 13:12).

1. "She was only twenty-three and supposed to be looking forward to some kind of great, adult life ahead, but instead

she felt like she was standing on the edge of a dock that hung dangerously over an acid-rain lake, which was normal in appearance and yet completely devoid of life. She didn't know whether she was normal or not. She just knew she was missing any significant sign of life" (p. 29). Does any of this sound familiar to you?

2. "Angie discovered the medicating value of sex" (p. 29). What is it about sex that seems to be so medicinal? What would you have suggested to Angie had you known her then? What would you have chosen to do if it were you?

3. Angie feels sad . . . overwhelmingly so. Does this feeling make sense to you, given what you know of her life? What other kinds of feelings would you expect from her? How would you respond to such sadness?

4. Why do you think Angie takes Emil up on his offer to talk?

Session 4

Chapter 8

... in which Angie and Emil have an important conversation.

*"Why, O Lord, do you stand far off? Why do you hide your-
self in times of trouble?" (Psalm 10:1).*

1. What do you think is Emil's "agenda" in his conversation with
   Angie? Why is he there? What is he hoping will happen?

2. What does Emil do in order to build trust with Angie? How
   would you characterize his conversation style?

3. Where has God been in Angie's life? Do you understand or
   share her frustrations at the apparent absence of God during
   times of pain and despair? What would you say to Angie
   about God if you were on the other side of the table?

4. Why is Angie uncomfortable around Pastor Paul and the others from the church?

Chapter 9

. . . in which Paul anticipates his conversation with Emil.

"O Lord, I am ashamed and confused before your face"
(I Esdras 8:74).

1. Paul finds Emil to be paradoxical . . . he doesn't fit into a "box." What are your boxes? What box do you have Emil in? Paul? Angie? Yourself?

2. Do you agree with Paul that evangelistic efforts by Christians just don't seem to have great effect anymore? Do you see something that is "working" well?

3. What does Paul mean: "What if we don't have the story right?"

Chapter 10

... in which we see Emil at home.

"The prophet is a fool, the man of the spirit is mad!"
(Hosea 9:7).

1. What is Emil doing? What does it say about him?

2. And how do you feel about it?

Session 5

Chapter 11

... in which Angie has a nightmare.

*"Death shall be their shepherd; straight to the grave
they descend" (Psalm 49:14).*

1. Angie's nightmare is a fairly common dream of "falling."
   Have you had any similar dreams? How did you feel?

2. If you were Angie, how would you interpret this dream?

Chapter 12

... in which Paul makes a surprising discovery about Emil.

"Did not our hearts burn within us ... ?" (Luke 24:32).

1. Emil considers talking with and listening to people as something he does . . . part of his adventure and not just his job. To what extent is this part of your adventure as well?

2. Did you notice that in Chapter 9 Paul is trying to figure out what box Emil is in . . . and now in chapter 12 Emil is trying to figure out which box (denominationally-speaking) Paul is in? We pick up a lot of cues about people by how they dress, what they drink, etc. And sometimes get them wrong, don't we?

3. Emil doesn't want to be considered a "Christian." Why? What does he mean by "follower of Jesus"? How is this different?

4. So what is the good news, according to Emil? And if he's right, what does that mean for our evangelism?

5. Emil says at the end of the chapter that the good news is not just about talking. "It's also about being present to people. It's about demonstrating to people that God's kingdom is here and that God is at work" (p. 49). How do you do that?

Chapter 13

. . . in which Angie tells Emil some surprising news.

"In you the orphan finds mercy" (Hosea 14:3).

1. Emil says, "I think dreams do mean something once in a
   while" (p. 51). What about you? Do you think they mean
   something? If so, how can you know what? And to whom?

2. Why is Emil prepared to suggest that the person in the
   elevator with Angie might be God?

3. Why is Angie prepared to discuss this dream . . . and to
   reveal her deep secret . . . to Emil?

SESSION 6

Chapter 14

... in which Paul and Dean discuss grace ... and Gracie.

"Where were you when I laid the foundation of the earth?"
(Job 38:4).

1. Paul contrasts two images of Christianity (p. 54) ... one a circle with those who are "in" and those who are "out," and one a process (a journey? pilgrimage?) of different stages, different paces, and different ways. Which of these images makes most sense to you? Do you have another preferred image?

2. How has Dean's ethnic and social background affected his theological questions? His ministry choices?

3. What does John Wesley mean by prevenient grace? How would you respond to that idea?

4. What kind of emotional reaction do you have to Gracie's note? Did it sound familiar? What is she up to?

Chapter 15

... in which Emil makes a promise.

"There is a way that seems right to a person, but its end is the way to death" (Proverbs 14:12).

1. Does Angie's elevator have to crash?

Chapter 16

... in which Angie makes a decision.

"But Mary treasured all these words and pondered them in her heart" (Luke 2:19).

1. Angie wonders, "Maybe life is bad but God is good." And, then, "If God was good, then why wasn't life good?" (p. 62) How would you answer her?

2. What kind of emotional reaction do you have to Angie's intention to have an abortion? How do you feel about Angie right now?

3. Have you ever had a glimpse of God . . . or a glimpse of something new about Him or His kingdom . . . that has been in anyway similar to her experience of "learning for the first time that there was such a thing as an ocean when you've always lived in the desert" (p. 62)?

SESSION 7

Chapter 17

... in which Emil does something unexpected ...
and invites Angie to do something too.

"So it is proof of God's own love for us, that Christ died for
us while we were still sinners" (Romans 5:8).

1. Reflect for a minute on Emil's reaction to Angie's decision
   to have an abortion. What does he mean by "participation?"
   Look up that passage about Simon of Cyrene and review it.
   How is Simon a model for those of who wish to share our
   faith?

2. Why does Emil decide to go with Angie? Could you do
   this? Should he? What does it communicate to her?

3. Have you done . . . or would you be willing to do . . . something like the exercise that Emil suggests to Angie? What are your desires? Obstacles? What would God say to you about them? How can your deepest desires lead you to God?

Chapter 18

. . . in which Paul, Dean, and Gracie have an online discussion about the Gospel.

"For the message about the cross is foolishness to those who are perishing but to us who are being saved it is the power of God" (I Corinthians 1:18).

1. The Bible gives us many metaphors to help us understand the atonement. These include justification, sanctification, atonement, illumination, awakening, ransom, reconciliation, adoption, redemption, and others. The point seems to be that the actual metaphysics of the atonement may be beyond us . . . all we know is that what Jesus did on the cross has something to do with our salvation. Some metaphors will better to you or me than others. Some seem to be particularly resonant at different points in church history. Which of the above words do you find yourself connecting to most often?

2. So Paul, Dean, and Gracie have a conversation that seems to end up focusing on the atonement. Paul is struggling with one particular model of the atonement. Which one?

Chapter 19

... in which Paul has a significant spiritual experience.

> "And as well as this, the Spirit too comes to help us in our weakness, for, when we do not know how to pray properly, then the Spirit personally makes our petitions for us in groans that cannot be put into words" (Romans 8:26).

1. And after the conversation he seems to find another theme emerging that he hasn't paid as much attention to? What is that?

2. Paul has more than just a cognitive experience; it seems to be a significant transformative "conversion" experience. What has happened to him?

Session 8

Chapter 20

. . . in which Dean and Gracie have a disturbing conversation.

*"Simon, Simon, Satan has asked to sift you as wheat. But
I have prayed for you, Simon, that your faith may not fail"
(Luke 22:31–32).*

1. Gracie's conversation really bothers Dean. Why?

2. Is this just his emotion or is there something wrong in her approach? Maybe you would disagree with Dean and believe that Gracie is doing the right thing?

3. What should Dean do now?

Chapter 21

... in which Paul gets an unwelcome email message.

"For if any are hearers of the word and not doers, they
are like those who look at themselves in a mirror; for
they look at themselves and, on going away, immedi-
ately forget what they were like" (James 1:23–24).

1. Things are escalating quickly now. How do you feel if you're
   following God in a new direction in your life . . . and finding
   consolation or joy in that journey . . . and find that others do
   not understand? Or will not understand? What are the temp-
   tations in such a moment? What is the invitation from God?

2. What are Gracie's motives? How is God looking at this?

3. How has Frank handled this situation thus far?

4. Note Paul's thoughts at the pub about Angie. What do he
   and Gracie have in common at this moment?

Chapter 22

... in which Paul's family talks about their feelings.

"Truly God is good to the upright, to those who are pure in heart. But as for me, my feet had almost stumbled; my steps had nearly slipped" (Psalm 73:1–2).

1. Sheila is afraid. Of what? Have you ever been afraid like this?

2. Paul is reminded of why he didn't want to do ministry in the first place. What grace does he need right now?

3. Lindsay speaks truth to her mother. What is the essence of her encouragement?

Chapter 23

... in which Paul has a tense meeting in his office.

"It is not enemies who taunt me—I could bear that; it is not adversaries who deal insolently with me—I could hide from them. But it is you, my equal, my companion, my familiar friend, with whom I kept pleasant company; we walked I the house of God with the throng" (Psalm 55:12–14).

1. Make a list of the things Gracie does wrong at this meeting. Why are they wrong? What are the biblical principles that support your assessment?

2. Make a list of the things Frank does right at this meeting. Why are they right? What are the biblical principles that support your assessment?

3. At the end, Frank observes, "Just remember, Paul. If the church succeeds—whatever that means—then we give God the credit. If it fails, then it's all your fault. Isn't that just a great deal?" (p. 96). Is that your experience or understanding as well?

4. What's the theological assumption underlying Frank's observation? What should we think about this?

SESSION 9

Chapter 24

... in which Angie and Emil both hear from God.

"The love of God is greater far
Than tongue or pen can ever tell;
It goes beyond the highest star
And reaches to the lowest hell"

—F. M. Lehman

1. What does Angie want more than anything else? What do *you* want more than anything else? Are you very much different from Angie?

2. What does Emil want? What does he do as a result?

3. "Lord Jesus, Son of God, have mercy on me" is a very ancient, Eastern prayer tradition. Known as the "Jesus Prayer," it's repeated over and over again, so that in the recital the prayer eventually emerges from the heart and not just the

words. It's a prayer of humility, desperation, and trust. Have
you prayed the Jesus prayer? If not, in preparation for this
discussion, perhaps you would want to take a little time (2
minutes, or maybe even 10 minutes) and let your tongue
and then your mind and finally your heart pray this prayer
to Jesus. Then come tell us what you experience.

4. What does Jesus mean when says he's got Emil's brokenness
and sin . . . and Angie's too . . . all over him? What emotion
does this release in you? What does this communicate to
Emil regarding his own participation in Angie's sin?

5. Angie is in the elevator again. But this time something different happens. Why? How? What difference does this make for
her? What does the knowledge of God's love for you do in
you?

Chapter 25

. . . in which Paul struggles with his own inner fears.

"Love never ends" (I Corinthians 13:8).

1. Why is it that kids think their parents are sexual zombies?

2. Paul realizes that while he might not do some of the horrible things that others might do, "the possibilities and potential for that horror are still there" (p. 107). He thinks that frees him to be with the broken, hurting, and sinful people of the world. He does such realization affect you? Free you? Trouble you?

3. "So does that mean that a Christian's life of spiritual formation should lead to just hanging around with people and smiling at their destructive lives, hoping that they'll finally catch on to what God wants for them" (p. 107)?

Session 10

Chapter 26

... in which Angie makes an appointment with Emil.

*"No one has greater love than this, to lay down one's life
for one's friends" (John 15:13).*

1. Is Emil "getting in over his head" (p. 108)? What would that look like?

Chapter 27

... in which Emil is watched in a waiting room.

*"As he came near and saw the city, he wept over it"
(Luke 19:41).*

1. The receptionist notes that guilt will give one a heavy weight to carry. But Emil is carrying another weight. What is it?

Chapter 28

. . . in which Angie finds herself back in the elevator.

*"I turned and gave my heart up to despair concerning all
the toil of my labors under the sun" (Ecclesiastes 2:20).*

1. Angie is in the elevator again. This time she sees a button
    marked "open," and she realizes that she might not actually
    be trapped. Why is she able to see and feel this now, when
    she wasn't earlier?

2. When the elevator door open, Angie finds herself some-
    place familiar? Where is she? And how does she know it?

3. Where is your home?

Session 11

Chapter 29

. . . in which Angie goes home.

"There is no fear in love, but perfect love casts out fear"
(I John 4:18).

1. Angie sees something in Emil's eyes? What is it?

2. And how does she know?

Chapter 30

. . . in which Paul hears from Gracie.

"I saw all the deeds that are done under the sun; and see,
all is vanity and a chasing after the wind. What is crooked
cannot be made straight, and what is lacking cannot be
counted" (Ecclesiastes 1:14–15).

1. Is this solution to the problem of Gracie too easy? Does it usually work out like this?

2. What should Paul do if Gracie were to stay?

Chapter 31

. . . in which Angie wants to talk to Father Tom.

"For this reason I tell you that her sins, many as they are, have been forgiven her; because she has shown such great love" (Luke 7:47).

1. Angie knows now that Emil loves her . . . but his love is being a bit pushy at the moment. She keeps asking for space. Why?

2. What is Emil not hearing or understanding? He is wondering where God is in all of this. Where is God?

3. Why does Angie want to see Father Tom?

Session 12

Epilogue

... in which things start changing at Music City
Community Church.

"The best way to know God is to love many things"
(Vincent van Gogh).

1. Gracie just disappears and Paul is disturbed. Why? Have
   you experienced or felt the same thing?

2. "Attendance at the Bible study eroded, but the ones who re-
   mained seemed to be very serious about their own spiritual
   formation" (p. 119). Thirty percent of the congregation left.
   How does that encourage or discourage you?

3. How does the story of the woman who bought flowers for a troubled stranger in the park illustrate these principles of the kingdom?

4. Paul started changing the rhythm of his own life, in order to incorporate time for devotional reflection and silent retreats. How does your schedule reflect this priority? How about your heart?

6. Emil encourages Paul that maybe he doesn't need a "hook" to hang the Gospel on when he talks to people. "It could be that you still see them as *ins* and *outs*; some people are in because they are in the church, or are Christians while everyone else is out. But don't we really believe that God's love is for everyone? Isn't that what Jesus was showing when he touched the untouchables and the outcasts" (p. 125)? Hmmm . . . how have you divided up the people in your world?

7. How does Emil describe Angie's current spiritual state?

8. What is the best way to love God?

9. Paul is pleased that his leadership team is willing to entertain new things, but is "somewhat surprised at their hesitation in letting the new things begin with them" (p. 119). At the end of this study, what new thing is God wanting to do among you that you find yourself hesitant to begin? How is God calling you to model, lead or initiate that new thing?

More About . . .

Michael McNichols, the author of *The Bartender,* is director of Fuller Seminary's Regional Center in Irvine, California and Adjunct Assistant Professor of Leadership there. He is author of *Shadow Meal: Reflections on the Eucharist* (2010) and a contributor to *Proclaiming the Scandal of the Cross* (2006). He holds a Doctor of Ministry in Leadership in the Emerging Culture from George Fox Evangelical Seminary. Mike was a church planter in Orange County, California.

The Bartender: A Fable about a Journey was published by Resource Publications, an imprint of Wipf and Stock Publishers, Eugene, Oregon, in 2008. It is copyrighted material and should not be reprinted without permission from the publisher. *The Bartender* is available through the publisher and through online bookstores.

Tony Blair, the author of this study guide, is Associate Professor of Leadership Studies at Eastern University and co-Senior Pastor of Hosanna! A Fellowship of Christians in Lititz, Pennsylvania. He, too, holds a Doctor of Ministry in Leadership in the Emerging Culture from George Fox Evangelical Seminar, where he was a classmate of Mike's. He is the author of *Fire Across the Water: Transatlantic Dimensions of the 18th Century Presbyterian Revivals* (2010) and *Church and Academy in Harmony: Models of Collaboration for the Twenty-First Century* (2010).

Hosanna! A Fellowship of Christians (www.hosannalititz.org) is an independent congregation in Lancaster County, Pennsylvania, whose identity is "breaking rules, breaking barriers, and breaking chains." Hosanna! has been exploring the relationship between spiritual formation and evangelism, in particular, which made *The Bartender* a very relevant text for discussion.

www.ingramcontent.com/pod-product-compliance
Lightning Source LLC
Chambersburg PA
CBHW070828100426
42813CB00003B/531